Statics (London) Ltd
41 Standard Road, London NW10 6HF

First published by Statics 1995

Printed in England by HPH Print Ltd, Royal London Estate, 29 North Acton Road, London NW10 6PE

ISBN 1-873922-48-5

STATICS BOOKS

what to do when you WIN THE LOTTERY

by Christine Whale and Michael Phillips

. . . HIRE YOURSELF SOME HELP AROUND THE HOUSE . . .

..GIVE YOUR BANK MANAGER A FEW
MOMENTS OF YOUR PRECIOUS TIME...

... SURPRISE YOUR HUSBAND WITH A LITTLE COSMETIC SURGERY...

... GET OUT AND SEE SOME LONDON NIGHT-LIFE ...

..USE THE LITTLE RUN-AROUND TO GO TO THE SHOPS...

... ORDER A BETTER CLASS OF TAKE-AWAY...

...INVEST IN SOME PRIVATE PROPERTY...

... SET UP THE TRAIN SET IN THE GARDEN...

... SIT BACK, RELAX, WATCH T.V. FOR A FEW WEEKS...

...LIVE OUT YOUR LITTLE FANTASIES...

...START A FAMILY...

... TAKE UP A HOBBY ...

...MAKE A FEW HOME IMPROVEMENTS...

... DO THE WORLD A FAVOUR ...

... BE PREPARED FOR ANY OCCASION ...

... REFUSE TO CHANGE YOUR LIFESTYLE ...

... UPDATE A COUPLE OF HOUSEHOLD GOODS ...

... GIVE SUDGELY-ON-SEA A MISS THIS YEAR ...

... PICK UP A LITTLE EXTRA AT WEEKENDS...

...TREAT YOUR PET TO SOMETHING SPECIAL...

...HAVE A CHANGE FROM THE FRIDAY NIGHT VIDEO...

...GIVE YOUR CHILDREN A HELPING HAND WITH THE HOMEWORK...

... GET THAT NEW CLUB YOU'VE ALWAYS WANTED...

...RENEW YOUR INTEREST IN THE GARDEN...

...BEAT THAT RUSH HOUR TRAFFIC...

... MAKE SURE THE NEW PLACE HAS ROOM FOR THE MOTHER-IN-LAW...

... ENJOY YOUR OWN PRIVATE HEALTH CARE ...

.. PICK UP A FEW NECESSITIES...

... GET INTO SHAPE...

... BUY A POOL FOR THE KIDS...

...SURPRISE SOMEONE SPECIAL...

...SHOW THE BOSS HOW MUCH HE'S
MEANT TO YOU OVER THE YEARS...

... REFUSE TO GET OUT OF BED EVER AGAIN ...

... GET YOUR DAUGHTER HER OWN BATHROOM ...

...PUT A LITTLE BIT BY FOR A RAINY DAY...

... HAVE YOUR HOLIDAY SNAPS DONE PROFESSIONALLY ...

... JUST SIT BACK AND ENJOY YOUR MONEY...

...SPLASH OUT ON AN EXTRA PINT'A...

... INVITE SOME V.I.P's TO YOUR GARDEN PARTY ...

... SPONSOR YOUR OWN ENDANGERED SPECIES ...

. . . PUT YOUR CHILDRENS SAFETY OUT OF YOUR MIND . . .

... KEEP UP WITH THOSE HEAVY METAL NEIGHBOURS...

...TREAT YOURSELF TO A LITTLE GEE-GEE...

...CHALLENGE THE PREMIERSHIP...

... SPEND ALL DAY BADGERING TELE-SALES PEOPLE...

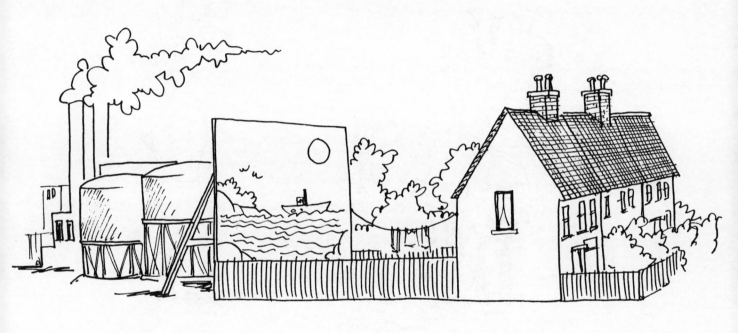

... IMPROVE YOUR SURROUNDINGS ...

... GET THE LEADING ROLL FOR THAT DARLING DAUGHTER OF YOURS ...

... SURPRISE SOMEONE WITH A LITTLE GIFT ...

...GIVE YOUR MOTHER-IN-LAW THOSE SIX MONTHS
WITH HER SISTER IN AUSTRALIA...

... DECORATE THE HOUSE ...

...PRACTICE YOUR POSE FOR THE YACHT CLUB...

... HAVE SOME PEACE OF MIND ...

... RENT SOMEWHERE FOR THE WEEKEND...

... MAKE SURE OF A PLACE IN THE SUN ...

... GET RE-ACQUAINTED WITH A LOT OF OLD FRIENDS...

... LAUNCH YOUR OWN PERFUME...

... MOVE TO A MORE SUITABLE LOCATION ...

...MAKE SURE YOU'LL NEVER BE FORGOTTEN...

... BUY UP EVERY LOTTERY TICKET COMBINATION ...

... GET AWAY FROM IT ALL ...